DOMESTIC DOGS
SHIH TZUS

by Susan H. Gray

Published in the United States of America by The Child's World®
PO Box 326 • Chanhassen, MN 55317-0326
800-599-READ • www.childsworld.com

PHOTO CREDITS
© Juniors Bildarchiv/Alamy: 9
© Kimberly Ryan/Associated Press: 29
© Linda Kennedy/Alamy: 11, 23
© Mary Altaffer/Associated Press: 15
© NDisc/Alamy: 21, 25
© Robert Dowling/Corbis: 13
© Tracy Ferrero/Alamy: 19
© Tristan Hawke/PhotoStockFile/Alamy: 17, 27

ACKNOWLEDGMENTS
The Child's World®: Mary Berendes, Publishing Director;
Katherine Stevenson, Editor

Content Adviser: Joe Walton, President, American Shih Tzu Club

The Design Lab: Kathleen Petelinsek, Design and Page Production

LIBRARY OF CONGRESS CATALOGING-IN-PUBLICATION DATA
Gray, Susan Heinrichs.
  Shih tzus / by Susan H. Gray.
      p. cm. — (Domestic dogs)
  Includes bibliographical references and index.
  ISBN 1-59296-777-9 (library bound : alk. paper)
  1. Shih tzu—Juvenile literature. I. Title. II. Series.
  SF429.S64G73 2007
  636.76—dc22   2006022640

Table of Contents

NAME That DOG!

What small dog is called a lion? ❧ What long-haired dog loses little hair? ❧ What dog has a beard and a mustache? ❧ **What dog is a favorite of emperors and everyday people?** ❧ If you guessed the shih tzu (**SHEE**-tsoo), you are right!

5

Tiny Chinese Lions

Shih tzus came from China. Nobody knows old they are. Little, long-haired dogs appear in **ancient** Chinese paintings. The paintings are more than a thousand years old. But no one is sure the dogs are shih tzus.

A few hundred years ago, Chinese emperors owned shih tzus. They liked these little dogs. The dogs' long, beautiful coats looked like a lion's mane. The name "shih tzu" means "lion" in Chinese.

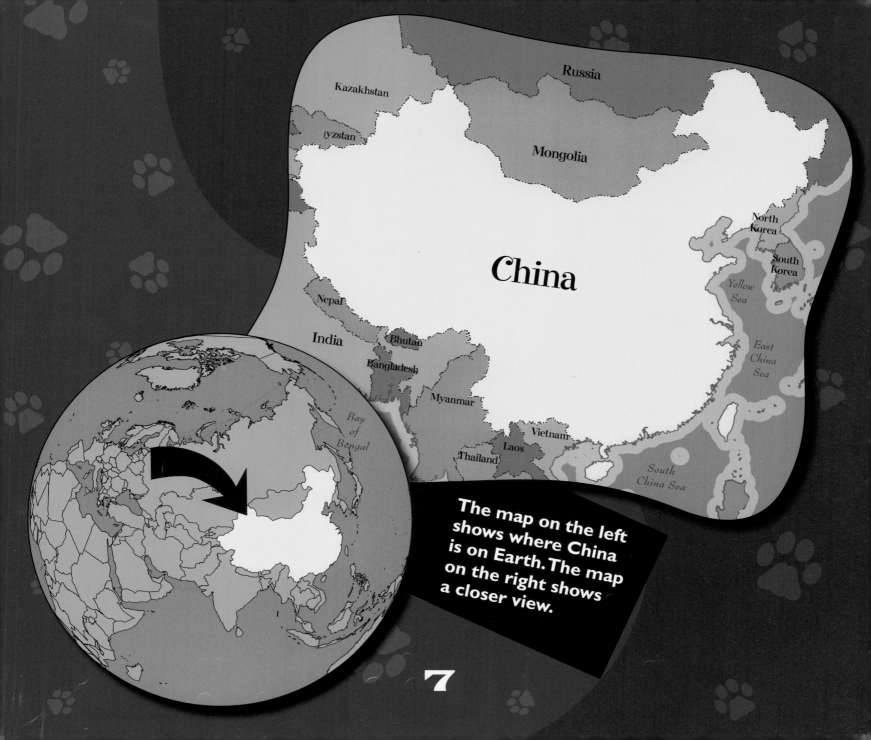

Kazakhstan

Russia

yzstan

Mongolia

China

North Korea

South Korea

Yellow Sea

Nepal

East China Sea

India

Bhutan

Bangladesh

Myanmar

Bay of Bengal

Vietnam

Thailand

Laos

South China Sea

The map on the left shows where China is on Earth. The map on the right shows a closer view.

7

Emperors were not the only people with shih tzus. Other Chinese families kept them, too. People loved these cute, friendly dogs.

About 80 years ago, a lady from England was in China. She saw shih tzus and liked them. She brought some back to England to live with her. Soon, lots of people in England wanted their own Chinese lion-dogs.

People who traveled to England wanted shih tzus, too. They took the little dogs back to their own countries. Soon, people began bringing them to America. Today, shih tzus live all over the world. They are one of America's ten most **popular** dog **breeds**.

Chinese emperors often had favorite shih tzus. They had artists paint pictures of them.

Shih tzus often tilt their heads when they are curious or are listening hard.

9

Small, but Good Looking

Shih tzus are small dogs. They are 8 to 11 inches (20 to 28 centimeters) tall at the shoulder. An adult weighs no more than 16 pounds (7 kilograms). That is a little heavier than a house cat.

These dogs have large, round heads. Their eyes are big and dark. Their ears are short and floppy. Their front teeth do not quite meet. Shih tzus are said to have an "underbite." Their lower teeth are in front of their upper teeth.

This shih tzu has had its long hair clipped. Shorter hair is easier to take care of.

11

Shih tzus are known for their wonderful coat. The coat has two layers. It has shorter, softer, thicker hair underneath. This is called the undercoat. Over it is the topcoat. The topcoat has long, soft hair. The dog's tail also has long hair. The tail curves up over the back. Shih tzus come in different colors—black, white, gold, and silver. Some are a mix of these colors.

The shih tzu's long hair covers its face. People say the dog has a mustache and beard. The hair hangs down over the shih tzu's eyes. Owners often tie that hair up in a bow. Then the dog can see! This little ponytail is called a "topknot."

Topknots are not just for looking cute! Both male and female shih tzus can wear topknots.

13

Dogs Like No Other

No other small dog has a coat like the shih tzu's! The hair on many shih tzus drags on the floor. It hides the dogs' legs and feet.

You might think that shih tzus lose a lot of hair. But they do not. That is one reason why people like them.

Their long hair needs work, though. It needs **grooming**. It needs to be combed and brushed. If it is not groomed, it gets dirty. It gets tangled.

This shih tzu is getting brushed for a dog show.

Shih tzus' small size makes them popular. These little dogs do not eat a lot. They do not need to run around outside for exercise.

Some people raise dogs they call "teacup" shih tzus. These dogs are so tiny, they almost fit in a teacup. But teacup shih tzus are not a real breed of dog. They are usually just the smallest dogs in a **litter**. Often they are small because they are sickly.

At dog shows, some people carry shih tzus on pillows. This keeps the dogs off the floor. Then their long hair cannot pick up dust.

Shih tzus are called "toy" dogs because they are small. Pugs and Chihuahuas are toy dogs, too.

Even shih tzus with short hair need to be groomed every day.

Puppies Are a Handful!

Shih tzu mothers have about three to five puppies in a litter. Sometimes they have only two. Sometimes they have as many as nine. Each puppy is small enough to fit in a child's hand.

The newborn pups are helpless. They have no teeth. Their eyes are closed. Their ears cannot hear. Their legs are short and weak.

This newborn shih tzu is only a few hours old.

As the pups grow, their legs get stronger. After a couple of weeks, the pups try to stand up. At first, they are too weak. But soon they are able to stand.

Soon, the puppies begin to walk and run. They do not run very far. They feel safer with their mother, brothers, and sisters. During this time, they learn to be with other dogs. They learn to be around people too.

The pups keep getting bigger and stronger. Soon they are ready to leave their mother. Most pups leave when they are about 12 weeks old. People take them to their new homes. They welcome them into their families.

This shih tzu puppy is about eight weeks old.

Shih Tzus at Home and at Work

Shih tzus were never hunters. They never learned to do hard work. For hundreds of years, people have kept them just as pets.

Today, shih tzus still make great pets. They are friendly and playful. They are smart and full of energy. Shih tzus love to be with people. They get along well with other pets. They like quiet children. They love having kids gently brush their hair.

Shih tzus love to run and play. This dog is playing with a toy on a sunny day.

23

Sometimes, shih tzus get jealous. They want to be the center of attention. They might not like homes with babies or small children. They do not like children who are rough with them.

Some people say their shih tzus are great watchdogs. The little lion-dogs bark whenever the doorbell rings. Sometimes they bark at strangers. But they can learn when to be quiet, too.

Some shih tzus work as **therapy** dogs. They visit people who are sick. When people are sick, cuddling animals helps them feel better. Shih tzus are cute and cuddly. They are small enough to sit on a person's lap. They can be great therapy dogs!

There are many different kinds of shih tzu haircuts. This dog's hair has been left long on its ears and legs. The rest was cut short.

Caring for a Shih Tzu

Most shih tzus get plenty of exercise running around the house. They do not need a big yard. They do not need to go for walks. But staying inside makes some shih tzus lazy. They eat and do not exercise. Then they get too heavy.

The shih tzu's long, beautiful coat can cause problems. It picks up dirt easily. If it is not brushed, it gets tangled.

Many shih tzus like to play with balls or other toys.

27

Bugs can hide in the dog's coat. Long hair on the dog's face can cover its eyes. Baths and brushing help. Haircuts help, too. The long hair can also cause ear problems. Owners need to keep the ears clean. A **veterinarian** can show them how to do this safely.

Many shih tzus snore. Some owners cannot stand the noise. Others like the sound. It tells them their dog is nearby.

Owners need to be gentle with their shih tzus. Playing too roughly can harm these small dogs. The dogs' lower jaws are not very strong. Dropping a shih tzu can hurt or break its jaw. Its eyes can be hurt easily, too.

Most shih tzus are healthy. Many live to be 13 to 15 years old. Some shih tzus even live to be more than 18. And they are lots of fun to have around!

This shih tzu is holding still while a veterinarian listens to her heart.

Glossary

ancient (AYN-shunt) Something that is ancient is very old. Small dogs appear in some ancient Chinese paintings.

breeds (BREEDZ) Breeds are certain types of an animal. Shih tzus and poodles are different dog breeds.

emperors (EM-pur-urz) An emperor is a man who rules a large area called an empire. Long ago, Chinese emperors kept shih tzus as pets.

grooming (GROO-ming) Grooming an animal is cleaning and brushing it. Shih tzus need to be groomed often.

litter (LIH-tur) A litter is a group of babies born to one animal. Shih tzu mothers often have four or five puppies in a litter.

popular (PAH-pyuh-lur) When something is popular, it is liked by lots of people.

therapy (THER-uh-pee) Therapy is treatment for an illness or other problem. Visits from therapy dogs can make ill people feel better.

veterinarian (vet-rih-NAIR-ee-un) A veterinarian is a doctor who takes care of animals.

To Find Out More

Books to Read

American Kennel Club. *The Complete Dog Book for Kids.* New York: Howell Book House, 1996.

O'Neill, Amanda. *Dogs.* New York: Kingfisher, 1999.

Soy, Teri. *Guide to Owning a Shih Tzu.* Chelsea House Publications, 1999.

White, Jo Ann. *The Shih Tzu: An Owner's Guide to a Happy, Healthy Pet.* New York: Howell Book House, 1996.

White, Jo Ann. *The Official Book of the Shih Tzu.* Neptune City, NJ: T. F. H. Publications, 1997.

Places to Contact

American Kennel Club (AKC) Headquarters
260 Madison Ave, New York, NY 10016
Telephone: 212-696-8200

On the Web

Visit our Web site for lots of links about shih tzus:

http://www.childsworld.com/links

Note to Parents, Teachers, and Librarians: We routinely check our Web links to make sure they're safe, active sites—so encourage your readers to check them out!

Index

About the Author

Susan H. Gray has a Master's degree in zoology. She has written more than 70 science and reference books for children. She loves to garden and play the piano. Susan lives in Cabot, Arkansas, with her husband Michael and many pets.